Francis Frith's
AROUND READING

PHOTOGRAPHIC MEMORIES

Francis Frith's
AROUND READING

◆

Martin Andrew

FRITH
BOOK CO

First published in the United Kingdom in 1999 by
Frith Book Company Ltd

Hardback Reprinted in 2000
ISBN 1-85937-087-X

Paperback Edition 2000
ISBN 1-85937-238-4

British Library Cataloguing in Publication Data

Around Reading
Martin Andrew

Frith Book Company Ltd
Frith's Barn, Teffont,
Salisbury, Wiltshire SP3 5QP
Tel: +44 (0) 1722 716 376
Email: info@frithbook.co.uk
www.frithbook.co.uk

Printed and bound in Great Britain

AS WITH ANY HISTORICAL DATABASE THE FRITH ARCHIVE IS CONSTANTLY BEING CORRECTED AND IMPROVED
AND THE PUBLISHERS WOULD WELCOME INFORMATION ON OMISSIONS OR INACCURACIES

CONTENTS

FRANCIS FRITH: *Victorian Pioneer*

FRANCIS FRITH, Victorian founder of the world-famous photographic archive, was a complex and multitudinous man. A devout Quaker and a highly successful Victorian businessman, he was both philosophic by nature and pioneering in outlook.

By 1855 Francis Frith had already established a wholesale grocery business in Liverpool, and sold it for the astonishing sum of £200,000, which is the equivalent today of over £15,000,000. Now a multi-millionaire, he was able to indulge his passion for travel. As a child he had pored over travel books written by early explorers, and his fancy and imagination had been stirred by family holidays to the sublime mountain regions of Wales and Scotland. 'What a land of spirit-stirring and enriching scenes and places!' he had written. He was to return to these scenes of grandeur in later years to 'recapture the thousands of vivid and tender memories', but with a different purpose. Now in his thirties, and captivated by the new science of photography, Frith set out on a series of pioneering journeys to the Nile regions that occupied him from 1856 until 1860.

INTRIGUE AND ADVENTURE

He took with him on his travels a specially-designed wicker carriage that acted as both dark-room and sleeping chamber. These far-flung journeys were packed with intrigue and adventure. In his life story, written when he was sixty-three, Frith tells of being held captive by bandits, and of fighting 'an awful midnight battle to the very point of surrender with a deadly pack of hungry, wild dogs'. Sporting flowing Arab costume, Frith arrived at Akaba by camel seventy years before Lawrence, where he encountered 'desert princes and rival sheikhs, blazing with jewel-hilted swords'.

During these extraordinary adventures he was assiduously exploring the desert regions bordering the Nile and patiently recording the antiquities and peoples with his camera. He was the first photographer to venture beyond the sixth cataract. Africa was still the mysterious 'Dark Continent', and Stanley and Livingstone's historic meeting was a decade into the future. The conditions for picture taking confound belief. He laboured for hours in his wicker dark-room in the sweltering heat of the desert, while the volatile chemicals fizzed dangerously in their trays. Often he was forced to work in remote tombs and caves

where conditions were cooler. Back in London he exhibited his photographs and was 'rapturously cheered' by members of the Royal Society. His reputation as a photographer was made overnight. An eminent modern historian has likened their impact on the population of the time to that on our own generation of the first photographs taken on the surface of the moon.

VENTURE OF A LIFE-TIME

◆ ◆

Characteristically, Frith quickly spotted the opportunity to create a new business as a specialist publisher of photographs. He lived in an era of immense and sometimes violent change. For the poor in the early part of Victoria's reign work was a drudge and the hours long, and people had precious little free time to enjoy themselves.

Most had no transport other than a cart or gig at their disposal, and had not travelled far beyond the boundaries of their own town or village. However, by the 1870s, the railways had threaded their way across the country, and Bank Holidays and half-day Saturdays had been made obligatory by Act of Parliament. All of a sudden the ordinary working man and his family were able to enjoy days out and see a little more of the world.

With characteristic business acumen, Francis Frith foresaw that these new tourists would enjoy having souvenirs to commemorate their days out. In 1860 he married Mary Ann Rosling and set out with the intention of photographing every city, town and village in Britain. For the next thirty years he travelled the country by train and by pony and trap, producing fine photographs of seaside resorts and beauty spots that were keenly bought by millions of Victorians. These prints were painstakingly pasted into family albums and pored over during the dark nights of winter, rekindling precious memories of summer excursions.

THE RISE OF FRITH & CO

◆ ◆

Frith's studio was soon supplying retail shops all over the country. To meet the demand he gathered about him a small team of photographers, and published the work of independent artist-photographers of the calibre of Roger Fenton and Francis Bedford. In order to gain some understanding of the scale of Frith's business one only has to look at the catalogue issued by Frith & Co in 1886: it runs to some 670

pages, listing not only many thousands of views of the British Isles but also many photographs of most European countries, and China, Japan, the USA and Canada – note the sample page shown above from the hand-written *Frith & Co* ledgers detailing pictures taken. By 1890 Frith had created the greatest specialist photographic publishing company in the world, with over 2,000 outlets – more than the combined number that Boots and WH Smith have today! The picture on the right shows the *Frith & Co* display board at Ingleton in the Yorkshire Dales. Beautifully constructed with mahogany frame and gilt inserts, it could display up to a dozen local scenes.

POSTCARD BONANZA

The ever-popular holiday postcard we know today took many years to develop. In 1870 the Post Office issued the first plain cards, with a pre-printed stamp on one face. In 1894 they allowed other publishers' cards to be sent through the mail with an attached adhesive halfpenny stamp. Demand grew rapidly, and in 1895 a new size of postcard was permitted called the court card, but there was little room for illustration. In 1899, a year after Frith's death, a new card measuring 5.5 x 3.5 inches became the standard format, but it was not until 1902 that the divided back came into being, with address and message on one face and a full-size illustration on the other. *Frith & Co* were in the vanguard of postcard development, and Frith's sons Eustace and Cyril continued their father's monumental task, expanding the number of views offered to the public and recording more and more places in Britain, as the coasts and countryside were opened up to mass travel.

Francis Frith died in 1898 at his villa in Cannes, his great project still growing. The archive he created continued in business for another seventy years. By 1970 it contained over a third of a million pictures of 7,000 cities, towns and villages. The massive photographic record Frith has left to us stands as a living monument to a special and very remarkable man.

Frith's Archive: *A Unique Legacy*

FRANCIS FRITH'S legacy to us today is of immense significance and value, for the magnificent archive of evocative photographs he created provides a unique record of change in 7,000 cities, towns and villages throughout Britain over a century and more. Frith and his fellow studio photographers revisited locations many times down the years to update their views, compiling for us an enthralling and colourful pageant of British life and character.

We tend to think of Frith's sepia views of Britain as nostalgic, for most of us use them to conjure up memories of places in our own lives with which we have family associations. It often makes us forget that to Francis Frith they were records of daily life as it was actually being lived in the cities, towns and villages of his day. The Victorian age was one of great and often bewildering change for ordinary people, and though the pictures evoke an impression of slower times, life was as busy and hectic as it is today.

We are fortunate that Frith was a photographer of the people, dedicated to recording the minutiae of everyday life. For it is this sheer wealth of visual data, the painstaking chronicle of changes in dress, transport, street layouts, buildings, housing, engineering and landscape that captivates us so much today. His remarkable images offer us a powerful link with the past and with the lives of our ancestors.

TODAY'S TECHNOLOGY

Computers have now made it possible for Frith's many thousands of images to be accessed almost instantly. In the Frith archive today, each photograph is carefully 'digitised' then stored on a CD Rom. Frith archivists can locate a single photograph amongst thousands within seconds. Views can be catalogued and sorted under a variety of categories of place and content to the immediate benefit of researchers. Inexpensive reference prints can be created for them at the touch of a mouse button, and a wide range of books and other printed materials assembled and published for a wider, more general readership - in the next twelve months over a hundred Frith local history titles will be published! The

See Frith at www. francisfrith.co.uk

day-to-day workings of the archive are very different from how they were in Francis Frith's time: imagine the herculean task of sorting through eleven tons of glass negatives as Frith had to do to locate a particular sequence of pictures! Yet the archive still prides itself on maintaining the same high standards of excellence laid down by Francis Frith, including the painstaking cataloguing and indexing of every view.

It is curious to reflect on how the internet now allows researchers in America and elsewhere greater instant access to the archive than Frith himself ever enjoyed. Many thousands of individual views can be called up on screen within seconds on one of the Frith internet sites, enabling people living continents away to revisit the streets of their ancestral home town, or view places in Britain where they have enjoyed holidays. Many overseas researchers welcome the chance to view special theme selections, such as transport, sports, costume and ancient monuments.

We are certain that Francis Frith would have heartily approved of these modern developments, for he himself was always working at the very limits of Victorian photographic technology.

THE VALUE OF THE ARCHIVE TODAY

Because of the benefits brought by the computer, Frith's images are increasingly studied by social historians, by researchers into genealogy and ancestory, by architects, town planners, and by teachers and school-children involved in local history projects. In addition, the archive offers every one of us a unique opportunity to examine the places where we and our families have lived and worked down the years. Immensely successful in Frith's own era, the archive is now, a century and more on, entering a new phase of popularity.

THE PAST IN TUNE WITH THE FUTURE

Historians consider the Francis Frith Collection to be of prime national importance. It is the only archive of its kind remaining in private ownership and has been valued at a million pounds. However, this figure is now rapidly increasing as digital technology enables more and more people around the world to enjoy its benefits.

Francis Frith's archive is now housed in an historic timber barn in the beautiful village of Teffont in Wiltshire. Its founder would not recognize the archive office as it is today. In place of the many thousands of dusty boxes containing glass plate negatives and an all-pervading odour of photographic chemicals, there are now ranks of computer screens. He would be amazed to watch his images travelling round the world at unimaginable speeds through network and internet lines.

The archive's future is both bright and exciting. Francis Frith, with his unshakeable belief in making photographs available to the greatest number of people, would undoubtedly approve of what is being done today with his lifetime's work. His photographs, depicting our shared past, are now bringing pleasure and enlightenment to millions around the world a century and more after his death.

READING – *An Introduction*

MENTION THE TOWN of Reading to many people and they think of Oscar Wilde's 'Ballad of Reading Gaol', or tell you that the town is impossible to get into by car, or that the middle has all gone and it is just a doughnut with a ring road and vast suburbs. Reading Gaol does survive, and possibly so do the very prison bars through which Oscar peered disconsolate. It is true that motor traffic makes life difficult and that many wrong planning decisions were made; but there were and are so many vehicles trying to get into, out of or around Reading that something had to be done. The villages around also suffer; Sonning is possibly the most put upon, as it serves as an eastern by-pass. Heaven knows how many vehicles pass over its narrow 18th-century bridge over the Thames. The river is the problem: there are very few river crossings, and it has been a subject of debate for centuries, not just recently.

However, after all that doom and gloom, I thoroughly recommend this somewhat misjudged town. The best way to see its architecture is to go on a Sunday, for you stand a chance of parking then, or to travel by train. The key to enjoying the town is to walk around the town centre and absorb its wonderful range of buildings from all periods of the town's long and fascinating history. Chapters 1 and 2 give an itinerary which is easily walkable, and which will give a feel for the town's morphology - that is, its evolution and layout. Chapter 3 looks at specific buildings and can be tied into the other chapters, while Chapter 4 moves down to the River Thames and Caversham, again written in the order of a walkable route, invariably the best way to immerse yourself in a town or area. The last chapter is to be seen as a car or bicycle route that takes in villages, locks and watermills along the River Thames from Pangbourne to Wargrave, with a couple of outliers south of the town.

The first documentary reference to Reading is found in The Anglo-Saxon Chronicle, which also refers to Englefield, near Theale (chapter 5). '871 AD: In this year rode the host [the Danish army] to Reading in Wessex ... then ealdorman Aethelwulf opposed them at Englefield and fought against them and won the victory. Four days afterwards king Aethelred, and Alfred (the Great) his brother, led great levies there to

Reading, and fought against the host; and great slaughter was made there on either side, and ealdorman Aethelwulf was slain, and the Danes had possession of the field of slaughter'. Thus Reading was precipitated into written history. The Danish army stayed in Reading over the winter, and having thoroughly pillaged the whole area, moved in 872 AD on London. In 1006 the Chronicle describes with grim humour another Danish army moving from the Isle of Wight to 'their well stocked food depot at Reading, and as usual kindled their beacons' - in other words, they burned every town and village they passed through.

Clearly Reading was a significant settlement of strategic importance, dominating as it did the valley of the River Thames and Kennet, and was well worth sacking. It was certainly an Anglo-Saxon borough or 'burh', and its Domesday Book entry tells us that it had a market and its own mint for coinage; pennies from Edward the Confessor's reign are known. Of the Saxon town nothing survives, but its location on a ridge between the marshy meadows of the Thames to the north and the

River Kennet to the south on its way to meeting the Thames is obviously defensible.

After the Norman Conquest of 1066, Reading emerges from obscurity with the founding of Reading Abbey in 1121 by the Norman warrior king, Henry I, nicknamed 'Beauclerc' because he, unlike most nobles, could actually sign his own name. Grieving over the loss of his son and heir in the White Ship, Henry invited the Cluniac order of monks to Reading and showered the new monastery with land and gifts, although at some time in the 13th century it became a Benedictine abbey. Work started immediately, and by Henry's death it was sufficiently complete, at least at the east end, for him to be buried before the high altar in January 1136. The abbey church, four hundred and fifty feet long, and built in the round-arched Norman style, was complete by 1164. A new Lady Chapel was added in the early 14th century. Until the monasteries were dissolved by Henry VIII in 1539 it was one of the most powerful and rich in England. The last Abbot, Hugh Faringdon, a former friend of Henry VIII, was hung, drawn and quartered for high

treason in November 1539 because he would not acknowledge the king's supremacy over the Pope.

This was a tragic end to a great abbey. One can only get a flavour of its scale, for most of it has been carried away over the years for building materials, including for the rebuilding of St Mary's church in St Mary's Butts in the 1550s. What does survive, however, is impressive: the towering flint core of the south transept walls and east chapel, the doorway into the cloister from the nave, the chapter house, and some of the buildings along the east wall of the cloister east walk. These have all been robbed of almost every piece of dressed stone cladding, so that what you see is the flint core of the walls, which were massively thick. Immediately south of the ruins the land drops to the River Kennet, which demonstrates how the abbey was positioned on high ground to the east of the pre-existing town. Elsewhere, fragments remain; but the gatehouse from the outer court, now Forbury Gardens, into the monastic precinct survives complete, although it was substantially rebuilt after partial collapse in 1861.

The Abbey was the only part of medieval Reading to be defensively walled, and the growth of the town and its prosperity owed much to the wealthy abbey. The town developed a strong wool and cloth trade which declined from the 17th century on, although sail making and a silk industry maintained the link with textiles for many years. It was also a market centre for a wide area, and took over from Wallingford as the county town of Berkshire.

Reading, with its strategic importance, had an eventful Civil War, changing hands several times. Indeed, it was the first town in England to be besieged, in April 1643, and extensive earthworks surrounded the town. The Royalists eventually lost, but there was much damage to the town, including the tower of St Giles' parish church which had been used a Royalist gun position. Of these defences only the tree-clad mound in Forbury Gardens remains. The Royalists had themselves blown up the nave of the Abbey church.

During the 17th and 18th centuries breweries, maltings, fulling mills and brick and tile making replaced the woollen cloth industry, and the town prospered and expanded. Mills, warehouses and industry developed along the Kennet; the river was canalised from the 1720s, despite riots and violent opposition, and later, by Act of Parliament in 1794, the Kennet and Avon Canal was begun. Completed in 1810, it led to new prosperity and expansion which shifted decisively northwards when the Great Western Railway arrived at Reading in 1840, later acquiring a huge goods depot and sidings.

In the 19th century, local entrepreneurs made fortunes and brought great wealth to the town. Many became household names, such as Huntley and Palmer, the biscuit manufacturers who, by putting biscuits in tins, solved the problem of keeping them fresh longer; Simonds the brewer, whose great brewery was eventually taken over by Courage in 1960; and Sutton's Seeds, which moved to Torquay in 1974. All this prosperity led to a building boom in the town centre in which many Georgian and earlier buildings were swept away, many in the interests of public health, for by this time these older buildings had become slums. Proud Victorian architecture can be seen all around: some, though, has been needlessly demolished to make way for the present scourge of towns, the motor car. But enough remains to give an excellent feel for this remarkably successful and wealthy town: McIlroys store of 1903, Queen Victoria Street (finished in 1903), Heelas store and numerous others. Many shops and buildings were rebuilt, often in the last two decades of the 19th century, in a Dutch gabled style: the soaring complex gables with pinnacles and the ball and other finials are mostly very visu-

ally attractive. All the same, the pre-18th-century street plan survives remarkably intact.

The town acquired a splendid Victorian Gothic Town Hall, designed by Alfred Waterhouse and built in 1875; a Corn Exchange in 1854; a covered market, later augmented by Market Arcade, a terra cotta and brick Jacobean extravagance which was severely damaged by the only German bomb that hit the town centre during World War II; and a Shire Hall for the County Council in 1911. Further out, a hospital (it was a notoriously unhealthy town) was built in 1839, the renowned Royal Berkshire Hospital, a Greek temple to the Goddess Hygeia; the town also acquired a workhouse; a gaol in 1844; and from 1892 a University.

I do not want to give the impression that Reading is essentially a Victorian town. There are many buildings from earlier periods, such as the medieval churches, including St Mary and St Lawrence; there is also a more unusual survival, the Greyfriars church at the west end of Friar Street. Admittedly, this last was ruinous and roofless by the time it came to be very heavily restored in 1863. It had been built between 1285 and 1311; the Franciscan friars' earlier site near the river on swampy ground proved too unhealthy, and had since the Middle Ages served a number of functions, including guildhall and prison. There are quite a number of timber-framed Tudor and 17th-century houses in the town, such as 27-28 Market Place. The Market Place also has a monument by the great architect Sir John Soane, erected in 1804, while the Forbury Gardens with their Abbey ruins are an area of calm and beauty.

The 20th century has done a lot of damage, particularly in the 1960s: for example in the Market Place, where multi-finned 1960s concrete awfulness intrudes, or the gruesome Broad Street shopping centre further west. The tide has now turned, but the town lost a great deal of quality then. I wish I could report that new building of more recent years has been better, but the bulk of it is - well - bulky, and often gimmicky. That is why it is essential to get out of your car to get the true character of the historic town, for the roads and underpasses that swirl round its periphery are lined with these new office blocks and prevent a true appreciation of the town's merits. These are considerable, and I do not intend to put anyone off: virtually all towns in England have made mistakes in the years when it was felt that total rebuilding and clearance was the only way to regenerate an area economically. Times have changed, and now I think the future of Reading's historic buildings is secure. The town's pre-18th-century plan has survived the deluge, the historic areas have been designated Conservation Areas, and the town has about eight hundred listed or protected buildings.

The book also looks in some detail at the River Thames, that great trade artery, now mainly a leisure one: its locks, weirs, watermills and bridges form the essential core of Chapters 4 and 5. Some of the villages in the itinerary are outstandingly pretty, such as Sonning and Mapledurham, but these few historic views are only a taster, just as with the views in Reading. For example, there is no view of Mapledurham House, or of Englefield's wonderful church of 1857 by George Gilbert Scott, or of Edwin Lutyens' Deanery Gardens of 1901 in Sonning or, in Reading itself, of the railway station, built in a delicate Italianate style in 1840. You can, however, see all these and many more by following the itinerary of this book with its historic views to set you on your way, comparing and contrasting past and present. I thoroughly recommend this very interesting town to you.

KING EDWARD VII STATUE 1905 37157b
The statue of King Edward VII was presented to the town in 1902 to commemorate his coronation. It is now in a busy traffic island, girt by flower beds, but it is remarkable that amid all the change and rebuilding Reading has seen the former Great Western Hotel, the statue and the Victorian station survive.

KING EDWARD VII STATUE 1904 52012
Our tour of Reading town centre starts at the railway
station, built in 1840 and remodelled in the 1860s.
Opposite is the Great Western Hotel, opened in 1844
and in an elegant Italianate stucco style. It is now
offices and the more architecturally robust 1870s
building to its left is now a theme pub.

ST MARY'S BUTTS 1912 64641

From south west of the station go first to St Mary's Butts, whose wide street was used until about 1600 for archery practice at the 'butts'. In 1886 houses in front of St Mary's church were cleared; the railings date from about 1890. Much on the left has now disappeared to make way for the gruesome Broad Street Mall.

SOUTHAMPTON STREET 1924 76246
Continuing south, past the modern Oracle centre and under the ring road flyover, Southampton Street has many early 19th-century terraces and also this 1873 church of St Giles by J P St Aubyn, utilising the medieval tower and aisle walls. The tracks belong to the town's electric tram system which ran until 1939.

OXFORD ROAD 1913 65912

As we return to Broad Street we see the huge building on the right, the former McIlroys, opened in 1903 and known locally as Reading's Crystal Palace for its huge shop windows. The top storey has been rebuilt in simpler style, but it is still miles better than the dreary Broad Street Mall that swept away all the buildings on the left.

BROAD STREET 1893 31721

Broad Street, formerly the sheep market when Reading was a prosperous wool town, became the commercial and shopping focus of the prosperous Victorian town. In this view, note the horse-drawn tram; the arched and pedimented building half way along on the left was the old covered market entrance, now brutally replaced.

BROAD STREET c1965 R13085

By the 1960s there has been much rebuilding, but Broad Street is still recognisable. The market entrance has yet to be demolished, and Marks and Spencers has not yet replaced the buildings to its left. To the right of the K Shoe Shop is a corner of Heelas' store, a noted local department store, now part of John Lewis.

BROAD STREET c1910 R13301

By 1910 the electric tram is operating, and the motor car has arrived to mingle with the horse carriages. The right-hand buildings lasted until the late 1960s when they were replaced by Marks and Spencer. Beyond the bank with its pyramid-roofed tower are the elegant terra cotta and brick buildings flanking the entrance to Queen Victoria Street.

BROAD STREET 1923 74436

BROAD STREET 1923

Further west, almost all on the right has gone, including A H Bull's French-influenced store with its steep pavilion roofs. In the distance is McIlroys' vast store with the name picked out in huge letters on the gable. On the left beyond Boots is the Broad Street Independent Chapel of 1892, now Waterstone's bookshop.

◆

QUEEN VICTORIA STREET 1910

Queen Victoria Street was cut through existing buildings to provide a direct link between Broad Street and the railway station. Relatively narrow between the tall ornate elevations built in red-orange terra cotta and yellow brick, it was the brainchild of a local businessman, Charles Fidler, who died in 1903 just before it opened. Fortunately it survives virtually intact.

QUEEN VICTORIA STREET 1910 62201

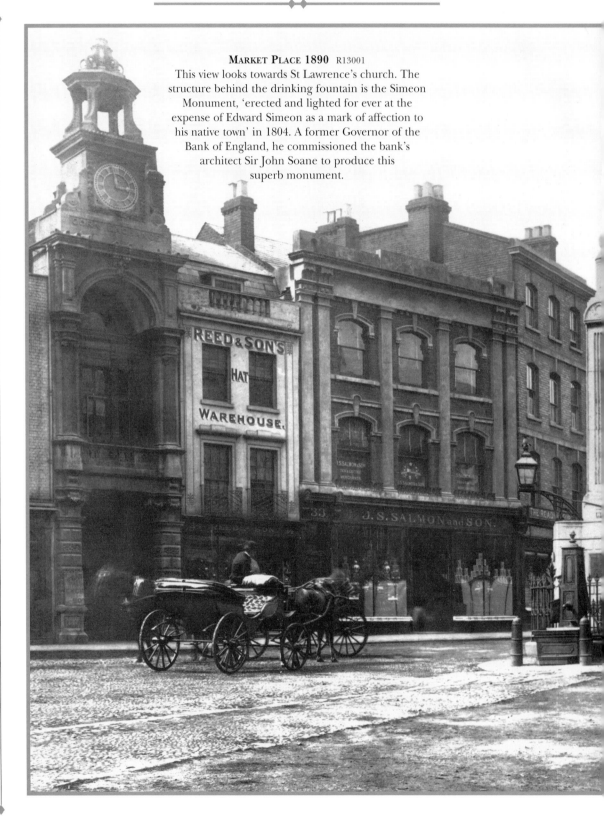

MARKET PLACE 1890 R13001
This view looks towards St Lawrence's church. The structure behind the drinking fountain is the Simeon Monument, 'erected and lighted for ever at the expense of Edward Simeon as a mark of affection to his native town' in 1804. A former Governor of the Bank of England, he commissioned the bank's architect Sir John Soane to produce this superb monument.

MARKET PLACE 1896 37156

The monument here is obscured by a cabman's shelter (better than the public convenience that replaces it now). The Corn Exchange entrance beneath its clock dated from 1854. J S Salmon has, since the previous view, extended his shop by another bay. Many of the right-hand buildings were (badly) replaced in the 1960s.

MUNICIPAL BUILDINGS 1893 31720

Round the corner from Market Square in Friar Street the vista is closed by the tower of St Lawrence's Church, complemented by the tower of the 1875 Town Hall. The Victorian corporation, in common with towns up and down the country from Manchester to Newbury, chose the Gothic style to suitably reflect civic dignity and prosperity.

FRIAR STREET 1924 76241

In 1922 the Post Office built one of its well-designed Neo-Georgian buildings next to the London Guarantee and Accident Company on the left. It is now a Yates Wine Lodge. Across the cobbled street only the building for the then Reading Gas Company survives, central Reading's only World War II bomb having hit the area beyond.

FRIAR STREET 1923 74440

The curious onion-domed extension to the Town Hall, between it and the church has long been demolished, but it serves to point up the quality of Alfred Waterhouse's 1875 Town Hall. Waterhouse was the architect of London's Natural History Museum and a Reading resident. The steep-roofed tower behind the chimney stack had at last been completed.

MARKET ARCADE 1896 37158
Reading's covered market was built in a landlocked site entered via the Corn Exchange from Market Place and the great archway from Broad Street. At the end of the 19th century it acquired this splendid arcade of shops off Friar Street opposite the Town Hall. Severely damaged by a bomb, its site is now occupied by Bristol and West House.

FRIAR STREET c1965 R13076
As we look west along Friar Street from in front of the Town Hall, the amount of rebuilding is evident: the occasional older building survives amid a lot of neo-Georgian dating from the 1920s to the 1960s. The Woolwich building survives, and the Arcade of the previous view abutted it on the left.

THE TOWN HALL c1955

In this view the right hand wing of the Town Hall has been demolished, and Thomas Lainson's 1882 wing can be seen at the left. Lainson was both judge and winner of the architectural competition for the extension! The statue of Queen Victoria was erected to commemorate her Golden Jubilee in 1887.

◆

FORBURY 1912

Moving east of the Market Place we enter the site of Reading Abbey. In the distance is the monastic gatehouse; the hipped-roof building is the former Shire Hall, opened in 1911; and in the foreground the semi-circular gable belongs to Sutton's Seeds, the world-famous company founded by a Reading seedsman in 1807.

THE TOWN HALL c1955 R13024

FORBURY 1912 64639

BERKSHIRE COUNTY COUNCIL BUILDINGS 1912 64640

The ball-finialled gate piers belong to the Crown Court's forecourt, a sedate Italianate stone building somewhat dwarfed by Hall and Warwick's confident Shire Hall built for the County Council. It is an exuberant William and Mary cum Queen Anne style building in brick and stone, and is now offices. Beyond is Sutton's Seeds and several houses, all now demolished.

KINGS ROAD 1924 76243

A longish walk east along King's Road leads to its junction with London Road and Wokingham Road. This view looks back towards the town centre with London Road to the left by the Marquis of Granby and the tram leaving London Road. The Co-op building on the right of 1900 survives, bereft of its tower.

THE ABBEY, THE CHAPTER HOUSE 1904 52018

THE ABBEY
The Chapter House 1904
Reading's great Benedictine abbey, founded in 1121 and completed in 1164, was one of the grandest and richest abbeys in all England. What remains is a gaunt flint mountain with barely a dressed stone intact. This view is within the Norman chapter house looking towards the entrance from the cloister.

THE ABBEY 1917
Of the great abbey church only the south transept and this arch, the doorway from the nave into the east cloister walk, survive. This view looks along the east cloister walk past the chapter house and, although it is only a remnant of the abbey, the towering flintwork gives some idea of the abbey's huge scale.

THE ABBEY 1917 67955

THE ABBEY c1955 R13021

THE ABBEY c1955

The abbey was built on the high ground north of the River Kennet, which in this view is behind the photographer. We are looking north-east into the cloister east walk past the refectory end wall. The ruins are a sobering reminder of the last abbot, Hugh Faringdon, who was hung, drawn and quartered in 1539 for alleged treason.

◆

THE ABBEY RUINS
A Fireplace 1910

This fireplace, possibly from the abbot's lodgings, was placed in the Norman south transept, but has since been removed to safer quarters. The abbey was dissolved by Henry VIII in 1539 and became in effect a stone quarry: some stone was used to rebuild St Mary's parish church, some went to Windsor Castle, and much else was used all over Reading.

THE ABBEY RUINS, A FIREPLACE 1910 62207

THE ABBEY GATEWAY 1896 37166

This splendid gateway was the inner gatehouse that led from the great forecourt, now partly Forbury Gardens, into the monastic precincts. In serious decay by the 19th century, it partly collapsed in 1861 but was reconstructed by George Gilbert Scott in 1869. Nowadays it leads into office precincts, rather than monastic ones.

FORBURY GARDENS AND ST JAMES'S CHURCH 1896 37168
This area survived as open space because the citizens
had rights to hold fairs and events in the former
monastery forecourt. However, by the 19th century it
had become a rubbish tip and dung heap; it was
bought by the Council in the 1850s to be laid out as a
public park much as it is today.

FORBURY GARDENS 1910 62206a

In June 1909 this memorial cross, seen here soon after unveiling, its granite pristine, was erected to commemorate Henry I, the abbey's founder, who was buried before the high altar in January 1136. Beyond is St James's Roman Catholic church of 1840, built in Norman style by Pugin, later a passionate advocate of Gothic architecture.

FORBURY GARDENS 1896 37167

Looking west past the Abbey gatehouse to the tower of St Lawrence's church, the photographer was standing on the site of the great Norman nave of the abbey church. Trees now obscure the church tower, and the gatehouse now has a higher neo-Georgian office block to its left.

FORBURY GARDENS 1890 27129

From a point further north-east, this view looks towards the gatehouse past the elaborate fountain which still remains today and the entrance gates beyond the thatched bothy, now replaced. The chimneyed building to the right of the gatehouse was demolished by 1904 to make way for the Shire Hall seen in later views.

FORBURY GARDENS c1955 R13057a
Here, just beyond the fountain, the bothy still survives, but with a tiled roof, while the Shire Hall, opened in 1911, with its balustraded hipped roof and built in mellow brick and stone, is now used as offices, for the County Council voted itself out of existence in 1997.

THE MAIWAND MEMORIAL 1890 27139

This extraordinary monument, with its gigantic lion snarling at the onlooker, was erected in 1884 to commemorate the sixty-sixth Berkshire Regiment's heroism and losses in the Second Afghan War of 1879 to 1880, particularly their rearguard action at Maiwand. In this view it is decked with wreaths and garlands for the anniversary.

FORBURY GARDENS 1904 52015

Although known as the Maiwand Memorial, it also commemorates the Berkshire Regiment's heroism at the Girishk and Kandahar, and records that eleven officers and three hundred and eighteen other ranks died in the mountains of Afghanistan during that terrible campaign.

THE MAIWAND MEMORIAL AND THE BANDSTAND 1904 52014
By 1904 a bandstand has been built near the Maiwand
Memorial; in this view the band's music stands are ready for a
summer performance. Note the policeman's summer issue
helmet, and the elegant white outfits and hats of the ladies.

THE MAIWAND MEMORIAL c1920 52014c

THE MAIWAND MEMORIAL c1920

After World War I the base of the Maiwand Memorial with its fluted pilasters and stone swags was rebuilt in a harder limestone, for the name panels had eroded badly. The names are now on bronze panels set between pairs of rather more restrained pilasters, and George Simonds' colossal lion looks equally at home on his new plinth.

THE MAIWAND MEMORIAL AND THE BANDSTAND 1923

This view shows the bandstand empty and the folding chairs used for concerts neatly stacked under a canvas sheet. There are fewer park benches now, and trees have grown up to obscure the view of the Henry I memorial cross on the right.

THE MAIWAND MEMORIAL AND THE BANDSTAND 1923 74441

St Mary's Church 1890 27137
This view, until 1886 concealed by houses, shows the tall, elegant west tower of the parish church now dominating St Mary's Butts. Although there was a Norman church here, it was mostly rebuilt with stone, flint and timber salvaged from Reading Abbey after its dissolution in 1539. The tower dates from 1550 to 1553.

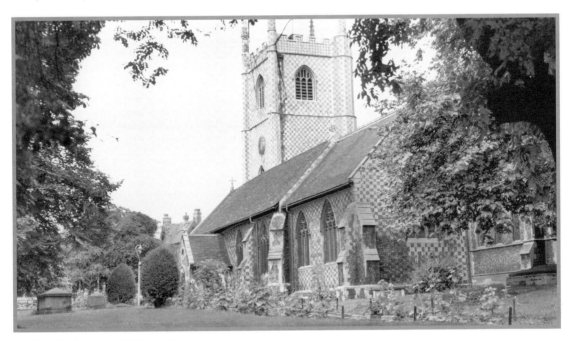

St Mary's Church c1955 R13056
From within the churchyard the chequer pattern of the walls is evident, with limestone blocks alternating with small panels of flint to give a rich decorative effect. Inside, the south arcade of the nave dates from about 1200, but the rest is from Edward VI's reign. Until its 1860s restoration there were dormer windows in the aisle roof.

GREYFRIARS CHURCH 1904 52009

The Franciscan Order, the grey friars, arrived in 1234 to a frosty reception from the Abbot of Reading Abbey, who grudgingly gave them marshy land by the River Thames. In 1285 the Archbishop of Canterbury intervened, and they were given this site; by 1311 Greyfriars Church was built. Ruinous by 1850, it was virtually rebuilt in 1863.

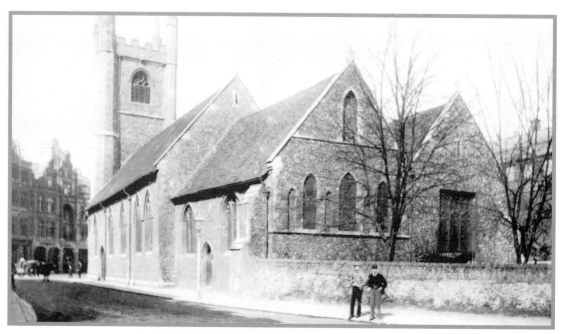

ST LAWRENCE'S CHURCH 1896 37159

This fine church at the top end of the Market Place was situated by the south gate of the Abbey. It has some Norman work, an east end with lancet windows of about 1200 and much other medieval fabric. The tower lost its pinnacles through bomb damage in 1943, which also destroyed Market Arcade in the distance.

ST GILES' CHURCH 1896 37161
St Giles' Church in Southampton Street was granted to Reading Abbey in 1191; it still has medieval fabric, in particular the west tower. The rest, including the soaring spire, dates from around 1873. During the Civil War the then spireless tower was used as a Royalist gun platform and naturally attracted damaging Parliamentarian bombardment.

ST GILES' CHURCH 1896 37165

ST GILES' CHURCH 1896
Inside, we see J P St Aubyn's rebuilding: a 'correct' Decorated Gothic-style east window and typical Victorian stencilled decoration, still very fresh in this view taken twenty-three years after its completion. Out of view are the numerous Georgian wall tablets and monuments transferred from the old church.

◆

ST GILES' CHURCH
Vicarage and Church Hall 1924
The old buildings in the foreground of the exterior view of the church were swept away and replaced by the well-designed Church Hall; in this view it has just had an extension completed, for its foundation stone was laid in March 1924 - the brick looks very clean and new. The vicarage beyond is now two private houses.

ST GILES' CHURCH, VICARAGE AND CHURCH HALL 1924 76248

CHRIST CHURCH 1896 37163

As Reading expanded south, St Giles', decaying and small, proved unable to cope, and Christchurch was built in 1861-2. It is a splendid example of High Victorian Gothic designed by Henry Woodyer, with a tower and spire 165 feet high. Alfred Waterhouse, who designed the 1871 vicarage partially visible at the left, also designed the Reading Town Hall.

CHRIST CHURCH 1896 37164

Inside, the church is a tour-de-force of Victorian inventive re-interpretation of the medieval Decorated style. Note the exuberant arcade capitals with their frieze of richly foliaged arches, and the reticulated tracery infill to the upper part of the chancel arch: Henry Woodyer obviously enjoyed himself when designing this wonderful church.

THE ROYAL BERKSHIRE HOSPITAL 1896 37172

Rightly one of Reading's best known buildings, the hospital looks more like a cross between the British Museum and an Oxford college. Built as a result of a vigorous campaign by a local citizen, Richard Oliver, and funded by public subscription on donated land, this great Ionic temple to health opened in May 1839.

THE ROYAL BERKSHIRE HOSPITAL 1912 64642

Although the 1839 hospital only consisted of the magnificent pedimented and columned centre block (on the left in this view) designed by local architect Henry Briant, it had expanded in similar stone wings by the 1880s. This view shows the grassed great court in front with its railings - they are now gone, and the forecourt is a car park.

UNIVERSITY COLLEGE 1912 64643

A little to the west from the Royal Berkshire Hospital, along London Road, are the buildings to which Reading University College moved in 1904 (from St Lawrence's Vicarage in Valpy Street) on land donated by Alfred Palmer of Huntley and Palmer's biscuit fame, one of Reading's major businesses. It was an electric tram ride from the town centre.

UNIVERSITY COLLEGE 1912 64644

In 1912 the college was an extension college of London University, which is how most of the 'red brick' universities started; it achieved independent status in 1926. Partly utilizing existing early 19th-century terraces and villas and building anew behind them, the university was soon bursting at the seams and acquired the Whiteknights site in 1947.

THE TECHNICAL COLLEGE c1965
Now entitled Reading College and Schools of Art and Design, and extended to the east, the Technical College was built on King's Road in the 1950s to somewhat mediocre and repetitive pallid neo-Georgian designs by Lanchester and Lodge.

◆

KENDRICK MIDDLE CLASS SCHOOL 1890
Opened in 1877, and still looking pristine in this 1890 view, the Kendrick's Boys School in King's Road was endowed by funds first established by John Kendrick's will of 1624. Kendrick had been a very successful Reading cloth manufacturer, and the original Oracle workhouse was also funded from his bequest; this is long demolished and its site is now the new Oracle complex.

THE TECHNICAL COLLEGE c1965 R13094

KENDRICK MIDDLE CLASS SCHOOL 1890 27151

COLEY AVENUE 1893 31722

Coley Avenue, running south from the junction of Castle Hill and Bath Road, was laid out along the great elm and lime avenue that led to Coley House, an 18th-century replacement for an earlier mansion. Although some of the trees remain, the massive 17th-century gate piers at the Bath Road junction, visible in the photograph, have gone.

PALMER PARK c1965 R13097

Palmer Park was laid out on land bought for the town by George Palmer in the 1880s, and his statue, formerly in the town centre, is now in the park. The park is just one of the philanthropic actions of the local 'biscuit baron' whose firm, Huntley and Palmer, revolutionised 19th-century biscuit manufacture.

PALMER PARK 1904 52023

This view of the Wokingham Road entrance is nowadays remarkably unchanged, apart from the loss of the lamps atop the gate piers and of the lodge cupola in the distance. As in earlier 1904 views, a policeman is in the picture wearing his summer issue helmet. The area beyond the gates is now a car park and bottle bank.

PROSPECT PARK 1904 52022a

On the west side of the town, north of the Bath Road , Prospect Park was bought by the corporation in 1901 'for the benefit of weary workers' through the efforts of its then owner Charles Fidler, the local entrepreneur who built Queen Victoria Street and Market Arcade in the town centre.

PROSPECT PARK 1912 64645

The park had focussed around Prospect Hill House, now known as The Mansion House, which after being a problem building for years is now a pub/restaurant with marvellous views south from its hilltop. The house, originally a brick one of 1759, was extended and given the Regency stucco villa treatment in the early 19th century.

PROSPECT PARK 1912 64646

The pond at the foot of the hill remains, although without lilies. It is heart shaped in plan, and was laid out by Benjamin Child, the then owner who stuccoed the Mansion House, in memory of his wife, Frances; it is claimed that she challenged him either to marry her or to fight her in a duel: a feisty lady!

ON THE THAMES 1913

Reading developed further south on higher land along the banks of the River Kennet, well away from the then marshy meads bordering the River Thames. Indeed, the only Thames-side development has been between Caversham and Reading bridges. This has conserved the openness of the river banks which play a central role in the town's leisure.

ON THE THAMES 1913

The land rises steeply from the well-treed north, or Caversham, bank of the Thames which is lined with boat houses, now rebuilt or gone, serving the prosperous villas and Victorian houses behind them. This view, taken from the south bank, has punts being poled and paddled, while people stroll and fish on the south, or Reading, bank.

ON THE THAMES 1913 65920

ON THE THAMES 1913 65919

ON THE THAMES 1913 65921

Further along, doubtless on the same summer's day as the previous two views, there is more boating activity, including a small sailing boat. In the middle distance is one of Caversham's big Victorian houses on The Warren, complete with a turret, a boathouse and its own river bank moorings.

THE RIVER AND THE PROMENADE c1955
This view, looking west from the present Caversham Bridge past the Reading Rowing Club behind the coach, shows well the flat south bank in contrast to the steep and heavily treed Caversham bank. The left bank was marshy meadow, but was bought by the council in 1907 and is now a public park with a popular riverside promenade.

◆

THE PROMENADE AND THE RIVER c1955
Taken from the south bank promenade, this view looks west past the eight-oar racing boats on their stands. The promenade was formerly the towing path for barges and boats with meadows to the south, but these are now tamed, and the southern part is now occupied by the very modern Rivermead Leisure Centre.

THE RIVER AND THE PROMENADE c1955 R13031

THE PROMENADE AND THE RIVER c1955 R13027

THE RIVER BY CAVERSHAM COURT c1955 R13040

On the north bank, the grounds of Caversham Court are now a delightful terraced public park; this view from the river bank looks south-east towards the 1926 Caversham Bridge, with the Thames Side Promenade and park seen in the previous two views on the right.

CAVERSHAM COURT c1955 R13039

Again in the grounds of Caversham Court, once the Rectory, this view gives some idea of the park's tranquillity, although the trees have been thinned out somewhat since. Caversham Court, which was near St Peter's Parish Church, was demolished in 1933, although 17th-century stables and garden walls remain.

CAVERSHAM BRIDGE 1904 52027
Caversham bridge has a long and complex history.
This view from the south bank towpath, taken before
its municipalisation, shows the 1869 iron bridge. This
replaced a curious one which was timber and iron
northwards to the then Berkshire boundary in
midstream, and stone for the then Oxfordshire north
half, the result of a cross border dispute.

THE CAVERSHAM HOTEL 1910 62208
A much changed view: this shows the old
Caversham Hotel on the Reading approaches to
Caversham Bridge, with the electric tram from
Caversham heading towards Whitley. The hotel
site is now replaced by a modern characterless
Holiday Inn; we may be thankful that the ornate
1905 drinking fountain has been saved and
relocated down by the river.

CAVERSHAM, BRIDGE STREET 1908 59962
Taken on the old Caversham bridge, this view looks into Caversham's Bridge Street with on the left the double gabled Taylor's Hotel of 1891; by 1908 it had been renamed the Thames Valley Hotel. The Crown Hotel on the right was rebuilt probably after the new bridge was erected in the 1930s. The tramway had not yet crossed the bridge in 1908.

CAVERSHAM, FROM THE BRIDGE 1890 27099
This view, looking east to the north bank of the Thames, has also utterly changed, for Freebody's Willow Grotto boat building business closed only in 1964 after hundreds of years on the site. It has all been cleared away to make way for blocks of highly desirable riverside flats.

CAVERSHAM BRIDGE C1955 R13048

Part of the 'deal' whereby Oxfordshire surrendered Caversham to Reading in 1911 was the rebuilding of the sub-standard 1869 bridge. World War I delayed proceedings until 1924, when work started on the reinforced concrete bridge. It was formally opened by King George V in 1926, but many do not consider it as beautiful as the Reading Bridge beyond.

THE RIVER THAMES C1965 R13087

From the south bank of the Thames just beyond Caversham Bridge, this view looks south-east across to the Caversham bank's Christchurch Meadows riverside park, once owned by Christchurch College, Oxford. On the right is Fry's Island, still well treed today. The swans are still as numerous and always on hand to receive bread, particularly in Christchurch Meadows.

CAVERSHAM, CHURCH STREET 1908 59968
This view is taken looking north-east along Church Street from the corner of Bridge Street and Church Road, nowadays a very congested traffic-lighted junction. The shop survives, but with a modern shopfront and plastic windows. The terrace of 18th-century cottages beyond remains unchanged, while the right foreground shop was replaced in 1938 by a neo-Georgian telephone exchange.

CAVERSHAM, FROM THE HEIGHTS 1908 59960

This view from Caversham Heights, north-west of the village centre, gives a good impression of the scale of Reading in the Edwardian period and before Caversham itself expanded far to its north and west. The skyline today is radically different: here a few factory chimneys break the skyline, but now large offices and shopping malls dominate the middle distance.

ON THE RIVER 1904 52024

An interesting view from the south bank of the Thames looking east, before Christchurch Meadows on the left were made into a riverside park, and, more significantly, before Reading Bridge was built. It crossed the river in front of Tims Boatyard, the balconied and gabled building beyond the George Hotel sign.

READING BRIDGE 1924 76255

Reading Bridge is an elegant reinforced concrete one, with a single main span and Brunel-like arches on each bank. Opened in 1924, it is an examplar of what can be done in the material. Beyond is Tims Boatyard, and to its left the island and the channel to Caversham Lock: compare this view to photograph No 52024.

ON THE THAMES 1924 76256

East from the south end of Reading Bridge John Tims Boatyard building, with its punts and boats for hire, has now all gone, replaced by the less than wonderful eleven-storey Reading Bridge House. To its left is Kings Meadow with its 1902 swimming pool peeping through the trees, and further left is the weir by-passed by Caversham Lock.

KING ALFRED TRAINING BRIG 1910 62213
The sea cadets parade proudly at their headquarters
east of Kings Meadow on the south bank of the Thames.
Moored at the bank is their two-masted training brig,
and beyond are the river-front houses of Lower
Caversham. One wonders how many of these lads went
on to serve in the Royal Navy in World War I.

CAVERSHAM LOCK 1912 64648
A steam pleasure launch enters the lock, to the
interest of passers-by. The mid 19th-century lock
keeper's cottage was rebuilt by the Thames
Conservancy in 1931, as were many others in the early
decades of the 20th century. The lock has also been
entirely reconstructed, but at least the trees
on the right remain.

PANGBOURNE, THE VILLAGE 1893 31719

Our trip starts well upstream of Reading at Pangbourne. This view looks along Church Street to the junction with the High Street. On the left is the churchyard wall, but the pine trees have now gone. The church's best feature is its 1718 brick tower. The buildings on the right all survive, including the Cross Keys

PANGBOURNE, THE VILLAGE 1899 42997

Round the corner into the High Street is the bridge over the River Pang. Colebrook and Co across the river now has a flat-roofed shop building attached, but the 1900 oriel windowed and tile-hung building beyond is by the noted architect Leonard Stokes and is part of a good Arts and Crafts range of shops and flats.

PANGBOURNE, THE BRIDGE AND THE OLD GEORGE 1899 42998

Taken from west of the River Pang, this view in the High Street shows the wagon wash in action. The bridge has, however, been entirely rebuilt. Fernbrook beyond and the George Hotel remain unchanged. Beyond is the start of Whitchurch Road leading to the River Thames, first passing under the Great Western Railway main Bristol-London line, built in 1840-41.

WHITCHURCH, OLD TOLL GATE 1910 62230

The river is crossed on a toll bridge; this view shows the toll gate and cottage, the former now replaced by a booth and barrier ten yards beyond. It replaced a ferry by means of a 1792 Act of Parliament, and is still in use (10p for a car, pedestrians free).The present late Victorian iron bridge replaced the original timber one.

WHITCHURCH, THE ROYAL OAK 1899 43002
Further uphill is the village centre. The only casualty since 1899 is the wall on the right, sacrificed for road widening at the junction with Hardwick Road. Sellwoods on the left had only just been built. However in the way of such things, it is now an art gallery, and the Royal Oak pub beyond is now a house.

MAPLEDURHAM, THE LOCK 1890 27089
Further down the Thames, Mapledurham Lock by-passes another weir. The lock, its footbridge and the lock-keeper's house have all recently been completely rebuilt as part of a major programme of upgrading all the locks and weirs along the Thames above Marlow. This view is from the south just downstream on the Berkshire bank.

MAPLEDURHAM, THE MILL 1890 27091

MAPLEDURHAM
The Mill 1890

Mapledurham, with its great Tudor mansion and unchanged village, is one of Oxfordshire's most picturesque and historic ones. Its former watermill, also partly Tudor, is approached down a short leafy lane and has in recent years been carefully restored. This view above the mill is from the west: one hopes the water is not being collected for drinking.

◆

TILEHURST
Roebuck Ferry House 1899

This is one of many ferries across the river, now almost all gone. The ferryman's cottage remains, but is now inaccessible and very private, with the river path blocked by a gate to its east. Behind is the London to Bristol main line railway, and on top of the tree-clad river cliff bank is the Oxford Road.

TILEHURST, ROEBUCK FERRY HOUSE 1899 43007

TILEHURST, SCHOOL ROAD c1960 T48027

In 1911 Reading formally absorbed much of Tilehurst, which had already in effect become a suburb of the town. Its 19th-century expansion was very rapid; this view captures some of its rather mundane Victorian suburban development. The shops remain, but the trolley buses which arrived in 1939 did not survive long after this photograph.

SONNING ON THAMES, THE LOCK 1917 67959

Back to the river and downstream of Reading, Sonning Lock itself has been entirely renewed but the cottages remain. The lockkeeper's cottage had just been rebuilt in 1916 by the Thames Conservancy. Behind the photographer is the Reading Blue Coat School, founded in 1646, which in 1946 moved to Holme Park at Sonning from Silver Street in Reading.

SONNING, THE BRIDGE 1904 52035

This view is taken from the footbridge to the Oxfordshire bank. The fine brick bridge of eleven arches is 18th-century. More mature trees now conceal the view of the medieval church tower and of much of the Great House Hotel on the left. Traffic is an unbroken stream across the bridge: unfortunately, this beautiful village serves as an unofficial Reading eastern by-pass.

SONNING, THE VILLAGE 1904 52040

Fortunately, south of Thames Street you can escape the modern traffic. This view looks east down Pearson Street, with the High Street off to the left just past the cart. The best house in this view is the one with the diagonal chimneystacks, The Grove: it is Tudor, with an 18th-century pink-washed facade and a superb Queen Anne door hood.

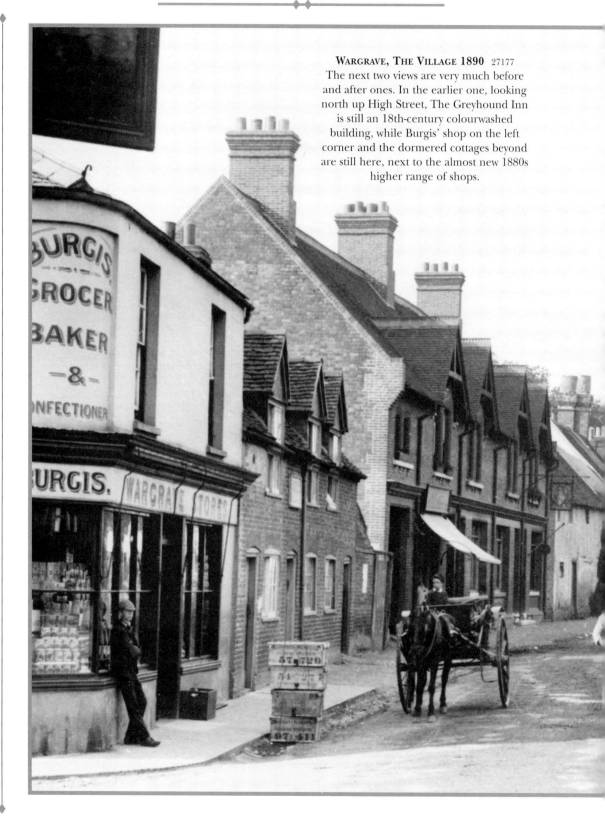

WARGRAVE, THE VILLAGE 1890 27177
The next two views are very much before and after ones. In the earlier one, looking north up High Street, The Greyhound Inn is still an 18th-century colourwashed building, while Burgis' shop on the left corner and the dormered cottages beyond are still here, next to the almost new 1880s higher range of shops.

WARGRAVE
High Street 1950 W25002
Around 1900, Burgis Stores occupied
rebuilt premises; so did The Greyhound.
Beyond the gabled shops on the left part of
Woodclyffe Hall is just visible, built in 1902
by Cole Adams in the Arts and Crafts style,
replacing the white cottage. The traffic is
now much greater - the High Street is the
A321 to Henley

SHIPLAKE, THE MILL AND THE LOCK 1890 27167
Viewed from the island in the Thames, this view is much changed: the lock was renewed in 1961, and Shiplake Mill has been completely demolished. In the photograph the mill's waterwheel is in a protective structure at the left. The mill house survives just out of picture to the right, but of the mill there is virtually no trace.

EARLEY, ST PETER'S CHURCH 1910 62210A
Leaving the villages along the river, we move inland south to Earley, now very much part of Reading. In 1910 Church Road was a country lane still. The church was built in 1844, with aisles and larger chancel added in 1883 as the population grew. A primary school followed in 1846, hidden by the trees to the left.

THEALE, ENGLEFIELD HOUSE c1955 T254016

About eight miles west of Reading, beyond the M4, Englefield House sits in extensive parkland grazed by fallow deer and beside a fine church by George Gilbert Scott of 1857. The Elizabethan mansion itself was fire damaged in 1886 and partly rebuilt by Richard Armstrong, who faithfully reinstated it for the Bunyan family.

THEALE, HIGH STREET c1955 T254001

The village lay on the A4 Bath road, but it is now a by-passed backwater with the roar of the M4 within quarter of a mile. Traffic levels are almost back to those of the 1950s. Little has changed, except that the brewery beyond the Bull Inn is now offices and housing.

Index

Frith Book Co Titles

www.frithbook.co.uk

The Frith Book Company publishes over 100 new titles each year. A selection of those currently available are listed below. For latest catalogue please contact Frith Book Co.

Town Books 96pp, 100 photos. County and Themed Books 128pp, 150 photos (unless specified). All titles hardback laminated case and jacket except those indicated pb (paperback)

Around Bakewell	1-85937-113-2	£12.99	Around Great Yarmouth	1-85937-085-3	£12.99
Around Barnstaple	1-85937-084-5	£12.99	Around Guildford	1-85937-117-5	£12.99
Around Bath	1-85937-097-7	£12.99	Hampshire	1-85937-064-0	£14.99
Berkshire (pb)	1-85937-191-4	£9.99	Around Harrogate	1-85937-112-4	£12.99
Around Blackpool	1-85937-049-7	£12.99	Around Horsham	1-85937-127-2	£12.99
Around Bognor Regis	1-85937-055-1	£12.99	Around Ipswich	1-85937-133-7	£12.99
Around Bournemouth	1-85937-067-5	£12.99	Ireland (pb)	1-85937-181-7	£9.99
Brighton (pb)	1-85937-192-2	£8.99	Isle of Man	1-85937-065-9	£14.99
British Life A Century Ago	1-85937-103-5	£17.99	Isle of Wight	1-85937-114-0	£14.99
Buckinghamshire (pb)	1-85937-200-7	£9.99	Kent (pb)	1-85937-189-2	£9.99
Around Cambridge	1-85937-092-6	£12.99	Around Leicester	1-85937-073-x	£12.99
Cambridgeshire	1-85937-086-1	£14.99	Leicestershire (pb)	1-85937-185-x	£9.99
Canals and Waterways	1-85937-129-9	£17.99	Around Lincoln	1-85937-111-6	£12.99
Cheshire	1-85937-045-4	£14.99	Lincolnshire	1-85937-135-3	£14.99
Around Chester	1-85937-090-x	£12.99	London (pb)	1-85937-183-3	£9.99
Around Chichester	1-85937-089-6	£12.99	Around Maidstone	1-85937-056-x	£12.99
Churches of Berkshire	1-85937-170-1	£17.99	New Forest	1-85937-128-0	£14.99
Churches of Dorset	1-85937-172-8	£17.99	Around Newark	1-85937-105-1	£12.99
Colchester (pb)	1-85937-188-4	£8.99	Around Newquay	1-85937-140-x	£12.99
Cornwall	1-85937-054-3	£14.99	North Devon Coast	1-85937-146-9	£14.99
Cumbria	1-85937-101-9	£14.99	Northumberland and Tyne & Wear		
Dartmoor	1-85937-145-0	£14.99		1-85937-072-1	£14.99
Around Derby	1-85937-046-2	£12.99	Norwich (pb)	1-85937-194-9	£8.99
Derbyshire (pb)	1-85937-196-5	£9.99	Around Nottingham	1-85937-060-8	£12.99
Devon	1-85937-052-7	£14.99	Nottinghamshire (pb)	1-85937-187-6	£9.99
Dorset	1-85937-075-6	£14.99	Around Oxford	1-85937-096-9	£12.99
Dorset Coast	1-85937-062-4	£14.99	Oxfordshire	1-85937-076-4	£14.99
Down the Severn	1-85937-118-3	£14.99	Peak District	1-85937-100-0	£14.99
Down the Thames	1-85937-121-3	£14.99	Around Penzance	1-85937-069-1	£12.99
Around Dublin	1-85937-058-6	£12.99	Around Plymouth	1-85937-119-1	£12.99
East Sussex	1-85937-130-2	£14.99	Around St Ives	1-85937-068-3	£12.99
Around Eastbourne	1-85937-061-6	£12.99	Around Scarborough	1-85937-104-3	£12.99
Edinburgh (pb)	1-85937-193-0	£8.99	Scotland (pb)	1-85937-182-5	£9.99
English Castles	1-85937-078-0	£14.99	Scottish Castles	1-85937-077-2	£14.99
Essex	1-85937-082-9	£14.99	Around Sevenoaks and Tonbridge		
Around Exeter	1-85937-126-4	£12.99		1-85937-057-8	£12.99
Exmoor	1-85937-132-9	£14.99	Around Southampton	1-85937-088-8	£12.99
Around Falmouth	1-85937-066-7	£12.99	Around Southport	1-85937-106-x	£12.99

Available from your local bookshop or from the publisher

Frith Book Co Titles (continued)

Around Shrewsbury	1-85937-110-8	£12.99
Shropshire	1-85937-083-7	£14.99
South Devon Coast	1-85937-107-8	£14.99
South Devon Living Memories		
	1-85937-168-x	£14.99
Staffordshire (96pp)	1-85937-047-0	£12.99
Stone Circles & Ancient Monuments		
	1-85937-143-4	£17.99
Around Stratford upon Avon		
	1-85937-098-5	£12.99
Sussex (pb)	1-85937-184-1	£9.99

Around Torbay	1-85937-063-2	£12.99
Around Truro	1-85937-147-7	£12.99
Victorian & Edwardian Kent		
	1-85937-149-3	£14.99
Victorian & Edwardian Yorkshire		
	1-85937-154-x	£14.99
Warwickshire (pb)	1-85937-203-1	£9.99
Welsh Castles	1-85937-120-5	£14.99
West Midlands	1-85937-109-4	£14.99
West Sussex	1-85937-148-5	£14.99
Wiltshire	1-85937-053-5	£14.99
Around Winchester	1-85937-139-6	£12.99

Frith Book Co titles available Autumn 2000

Croydon Living Memories (pb)			
	1-85937-162-0	£9.99	Aug
Glasgow (pb)	1-85937-190-6	£9.99	Aug
Hertfordshire (pb)	1-85937-247-3	£9.99	Aug
North London	1-85937-206-6	£14.99	Aug
Victorian & Edwardian Maritime Album			
	1-85937-144-2	£17.99	Aug
Victorian Seaside	1-85937-159-0	£17.99	Aug
Cornish Coast	1-85937-163-9	£14.99	Sep
County Durham	1-85937-123-x	£14.99	Sep
Dorset Living Memories	1-85937-210-4	£14.99	Sep
Gloucestershire	1-85937-102-7	£14.99	Sep
Herefordshire	1-85937-174-4	£14.99	Sep
Kent Living Memories	1-85937-125-6	£14.99	Sep
Leeds (pb)	1-85937-202-3	£9.99	Sep
Ludlow (pb)	1-85937-176-0	£9.99	Sep
Norfolk (pb)	1-85937-195-7	£9.99	Sep
Somerset	1-85937-153-1	£14.99	Sep
Tees Valley & Cleveland	1-85937-211-2	£14.99	Sep
Thanet (pb)	1-85937-116-7	£9.99	Sep
Tiverton (pb)	1-85937-178-7	£9.99	Sep
Weymouth (pb)	1-85937-209-0	£9.99	Sep

Worcestershire	1-85937-152-3	£14.99	Sep
Yorkshire Living Memories	1-85937-166-3	£14.99	Sep
British Life A Century Ago (pb)			
	1-85937-213-9	£9.99	Oct
Camberley (pb)	1-85937-222-8	£9.99	Oct
Cardiff (pb)	1-85937-093-4	£9.99	Oct
Carmarthenshire	1-85937-216-3	£14.99	Oct
Cornwall (pb)	1-85937-229-5	£9.99	Oct
English Country Houses	1-85937-161-2	£17.99	Oct
Humberside	1-85937-215-5	£14.99	Oct
Lancashire (pb)	1-85937-197-3	£9.99	Oct
Liverpool (pb)	1-85937-234-1	£9.99	Oct
Manchester (pb)	1-85937-198-1	£9.99	Oct
Middlesex	1-85937-158-2	£14.99	Oct
Norfolk Living Memories	1-85937-217-1	£14.99	Oct
Preston (pb)	1-85937-212-0	£9.99	Oct
South Hams	1-85937-220-1	£14.99	Oct
Suffolk	1-85937-221-x	£9.99	Oct
Swansea (pb)	1-85937-167-1	£9.99	Oct
Victorian and Edwardian Sussex			
	1-85937-157-4	£14.99	Oct
West Yorkshire (pb)	1-85937-201-5	£9.99	Oct

See Frith books on the internet www.frithbook.co.uk

FRITH PRODUCTS & SERVICES

Francis Frith would doubtless be pleased to know that the pioneering publishing venture he started in 1860 still continues today. A hundred and forty years later, The Francis Frith Collection continues in the same innovative tradition and is now one of the foremost publishers of vintage photographs in the world. Some of the current activities include:

Interior Decoration

Today Frith's photographs can be seen framed and as giant wall murals in thousands of pubs, restaurants, hotels, banks, retail stores and other public buildings throughout the country. In every case they enhance the unique local atmosphere of the places they depict and provide reminders of gentler days in an increasingly busy and frenetic world.

Product Promotions

Frith products are used by many major companies to promote the sales of their own products or to reinforce their own history and heritage. Frith promotions have been used by Hovis bread, Courage beers, Scots Porage Oats, Colman's mustard, Cadbury's foods, Mellow Birds coffee, Dunhill pipe tobacco, Guinness, and Bulmer's Cider.

Genealogy and Family History

As the interest in family history and roots grows world-wide, more and more people are turning to Frith's photographs of Great Britain for images of the towns, villages and streets where their ancestors lived; and, of course, photographs of the churches and chapels where their ancestors were christened, married and buried are an essential part of every genealogy tree and family album.

Frith Products

All Frith photographs are available Framed or just as Mounted Prints and Posters (size 23 x 16 inches). These may be ordered from the address below. From time to time other products - Address Books, Calendars, Table Mats, etc - are available.

The Internet

Already twenty thousand Frith photographs can be viewed and purchased on the internet. By the end of the year 2000 some 60,000 Frith photographs will be available on the internet. The number of sites is constantly expanding, each focussing on different products and services from the Collection.

The main Frith sites are listed below.

www.francisfrith.co.uk

www.frithbook.co.uk

See the complete list of Frith Books at:

www.frithbook.co.uk

This web site is regularly updated with the latest list of publications from the Frith Book Company. If you wish to buy books relating to another part of the country that your local bookshop does not stock, you may purchase on-line.

For further information, trade, or author enquiries please contact us at the address below:
The Francis Frith Collection, Frith's Barn, Teffont, Salisbury, Wiltshire, England SP3 5QP.
Tel: +44 (0)1722 716 376 Fax: +44 (0)1722 716 881   Email: uksales@francisfrith.com

---

See Frith books on the internet www.frithbook.co.uk

TO RECEIVE YOUR FREE MOUNTED PRINT

Mounted Print
Overall size 14 x 11 inches

Cut out this Voucher and return it with your remittance for £1.50 to cover postage and handling, to UK addresses. For overseas addresses please include £4.00 post and handling. Choose any photograph included in this book. Your SEPIA print will be A4 in size, and mounted in a cream mount with burgundy rule lines, overall size 14 x 11 inches.

Order additional Mounted Prints at HALF PRICE (only £7.49 each*)

If there are further pictures you would like to order, possibly as gifts for friends and family, purchase them at half price (no additional postage and handling required).

Have your Mounted Prints framed*

For an additional £14.95 per print you can have your chosen Mounted Print framed in an elegant polished wood and gilt moulding, overall size 16 x 13 inches (no additional postage and handling required).

---

* IMPORTANT!
These special prices are only available if ordered using the original voucher on this page (no copies permitted) and at the same time as your free Mounted Print, for delivery to the same address

---

Frith Collectors' Guild

From time to time we publish a magazine of news and stories about Frith photographs and further special offers of Frith products. If you would like 12 months FREE membership, please return this form.

Send completed forms to:
The Francis Frith Collection, Frith's Barn, Teffont, Salisbury, Wiltshire SP3 5QP

Voucher for FREE and Reduced Price Frith Prints

Picture no.	Page number	Qty	Mounted @ £7.49	Framed + £14.95	Total Cost
		1	**Free of charge***	£	£
			£7.49	£	£
			£7.49	£	£
			£7.49	£	£
			£7.49	£	£
			£7.49	£	£

Please allow 28 days for delivery	*** Post & handling**	**£1.50**
Book Title	**Total Order Cost**	**£**

Please do not photocopy this voucher. Only the original is valid, so please cut it out and return it to us.

I enclose a cheque / postal order for £ . . . .
made payable to 'The Francis Frith Collection'
OR please debit my Mastercard / Visa / Switch / Amex card

Number . . . .

Issue No (Switch only) . . . . .Valid from (Amex/Switch) . . . .

Expires . . . . Signature . . . .

Name Mr/Mrs/Ms . . . .

Address . . . .

. . . .

. . . .

. . . . Postcode . . . .

Daytime Tel No . . . .   Valid to 31/12/02

The Francis Frith Collectors' Guild

Please enrol me as a member for 12 months free of charge.

Name Mr/Mrs/Ms . . . .

Address . . . .

. . . .

. . . .

. . . . Postcode . . . .

Free Print - see overleaf